CELEBRATING
PRIDE AND
PREJUDICE

by Hazel Jones and Maggie Lane

Lansdown Media Ltd
17 Beauford Square, Bath BA1 1HJ

Copyright © Hazel Jones and Maggie Lane
2012

First published 2012

British Library Cataloguing-in-Publication Data

A catalogue record for this book is available from the British Library.

ISBN 978-0-9573570-0-6

Cover image
Colin Firth as Mr Darcy during the filming of *Pride and Prejudice* at Harrow School in 1995.

Designed by Walker/Jansseune, Bath, UK

Printed and bound by Blackmore, Shaftesbury, Dorset, UK

Contents

LANSDOWN MEDIA

PRIDE

AND

PREJUDICE:

A NOVEL.

IN THREE VOLUMES.

BY THE
AUTHOR OF " SENSE AND SENSIBILITY."

VOL. I.

London:
PRINTED FOR T. EGERTON,
MILITARY LIBRARY, WHITEHALL.
1813.

The World Loves Pride and Prejudice

Two hundred years ago a novel written in a Hampshire rectory and revised in a Hampshire cottage was published anonymously in London. Remarkably, from such quiet beginnings it has gone on to become a global phenomenon – its fame, popularity and influence on contemporary culture increasing with every decade. Even among non-readers its name is known; but to its legions of devoted followers it can seem like a private pleasure, shared with a choice few.

All the elements that have always been requirements for a good read are to be found in *Pride and Prejudice* – romance, angst, mystery, intrigue – and all expressed in clear, accessible prose, with rich seams of wit and irony running through. Comparing her "darling child" with the offspring of other fiction writers, Jane Austen must have realised that she had written something compellingly fresh, but could she have guessed that her fame would spread beyond the boundaries of the world she knew, that her name would eclipse those of the great authors of her time? The writer Fay Weldon believes that she could: "It may seem extraordinary that a brief romantic novel written by a 22-year-old girl in 1797 keeps making it into the lists of great masterworks … Pity Jane Austen if you must, this maiden lady without children or sexual experience. But she would have known the exhilaration of the writer when she put down her pen after *Pride and Prejudice*. I bet she knew that what she'd written would outrun the generations."[1]

What appeals to us today delighted Jane Austen's first readers too. Her characters are so substantial, so realistic that they step off the page into our lives and assume an existence beyond the resolution of the plot, and none more so than those in *Pride and Prejudice*. Jane Austen herself found it impossible to lay Elizabeth and Jane Bennet to rest. Four months after the novel had appeared in print, she searched

First edition
The title page of the first printing of *Pride and Prejudice* simply described the book as being by 'the author of *Sense and Sensibility*'.

It is a truth universally acknowledged, that a single woman in possession of a good fortune must be in want of a man who can take care of the kids, make a mean spag bol and still look like Colin Firth in a wet shirt which, after a night of ceaseless rapture, he will put in the washing machine and then iron.
Allison Pearson,
The Daily Telegraph,
April 12, 2012

for portraits of Mrs Darcy and Mrs Bingley in several London art exhibitions – and she didn't stop at those two Bennet sisters. Some time later she revealed to her nephews and nieces that Kitty married a clergyman near Pemberley and that Mary, content to be considered accomplished in Meryton circles, became the wife of one of Uncle Philips's clerks. It's hardly surprising that a search for *Pride and Prejudice* sequels on Amazon.com returns more than 300 titles.

Not only the characters are unforgettable – the opening sentence of *Pride and Prejudice*, penned more than 200 years ago, has become embedded in the modern collective unconscious. A tongue-in-cheek newspaper columnist, recommending 50 books not to read before you die, cites *Pride and Prejudice* on the ground that it is "directly

Global interest
Mugs from the US and bags from Brazil are among the legacies of the worldwide '*Pride and Prejudice* effect'.

responsible for too many newspaper articles starting 'It is a truth universally acknowledged ...'."[2] On an almost daily basis, examples can be found in the press or on the web: "It is a truth universally acknowledged that the media, in general, could do a better job of reporting science"; "It is a truth universally acknowledged that education is the key to economic success"; "It is a truth universally acknowledged that today's newspaper is tomorrow's fish-and-chip paper, but when it comes to Manchester United ..." Not one of the many examples on offer entirely achieves the elegant balance of the original; none attempts the deliciously ironic tone.

A BEST SELLER

Thankfully, the advice to avoid reading *Pride and Prejudice* before we die comes far too late for many of us. Since the novel was first published in 1813 it has only been out of print for a brief period in the 1820s and, despite Jane Austen's relatively slow rise to fame, every age has had its loyal *Pride and Prejudice* followers. Present day fans of a wet-shirted Mr Darcy and a feisty Elizabeth Bennet might have discovered Jane Austen first through film and TV, but a large number have gone on to appreciate her words on the page. The unprecedented popularity of the six-hour, 1995 BBC production, which attracted 10 million British viewers, fuelled the sale of 177,000 copies of the novel, making Jane Austen one of the best-selling authors of the 1990s. Since 2001, sales of the novel worldwide have totalled no fewer than 110,000 per year. The '*Pride and Prejudice* effect' has influenced the global interest in first-edition copies of the novel, which now sell for phenomenal sums of money. At the beginning of this century Christie's in London sold a first edition for £23,500; in 2009, a copy in original boards made £139,000.

Added to the literary and film enthusiasts are the *Pride and Prejudice* tourists and website creators, the bloggers and tweeters, the prequel and sequel writers, the wearers of "What do you mean, Mr Darcy isn't real?" T-shirts and the collectors of "I ♥ Darcy" car stickers, "I'd rather be at Pemberley" fridge magnets and "How shall I bear so much happiness" mugs. Recently on the market is a five-inch vinyl 'action figure' of Jane Austen, complete with writing desk, quill pen and a mini copy of *Pride and Prejudice*. And hands up all those with the 1995 *Pride and Prejudice* theme tune as a mobile phone ring-tone. Two centuries after the London publisher Thomas Cadell turned down this work of genius, sight unseen, it is, in all its manifestations, a globally acknowledged big earner.

Jane Austen Sociedade do Brasil

UNIVERSAL FAME

The novel's universal appeal stretches from Norway to Nigeria, from Spain to Siberia, thanks in part to visual representations, but also to the proliferation in the 20th century of translations into other languages. There are currently six Japanese versions of *Pride and Prejudice*, the most frequently taught Austen novel in Japan. One intrepid professor from the University of the Pacific recently travelled the length and breadth of Latin America conducting reading groups in Guatemala, Mexico, Paraguay and Argentina. "Readers in those countries love Jane Austen," she reported. She discovered that *Pride and Prejudice* had a particular resonance for those readers who had experienced racially motivated civil strife. The City page of *The Times of India*, for January 28, 2012, celebrated the advent of the novel's 200th year, praising it as "a book that's vibrantly alive on screen, on tube and on bookshelves". Under the headline "Jane Austen scores a double ton", the article goes on: "*Pride and Prejudice* continues to fascinate, with soaps and big screen adaptations *de rigueur*, even in India." On the same page is a review of P. D. James's sequel, *Death Comes to Pemberley*.

Jane Austen societies exist in the UK, Italy, the Netherlands, North America, Australia, Japan, Brazil and Argentina. At US conventions in particular, Regency costumes are donned at the drop of a bonnet. Transformed into Lizzys, Lady Catherines, Mrs Bennets and Miss Bingleys, members of the Jane Austen Society of North America listen to eminent speakers, take tea and attend period balls. Dressing the part is every Austen lover's dream, whether in secret or unashamedly acknowledged. Groups and individuals from all over the world descend on Bath, England, every September for the annual Jane Austen Festival to promenade around the Circus and along Royal Crescent in their fine spotted muslins, dashing militia uniforms and fashionable cut-away coats. Yes, Jane has her male following too, and we can make a fairly accurate guess at her response to these handsome modern men in Mr Darcy jackets or Mr Wickham regimentals.

Some of her most illustrious male readers were statesmen. In the past century two British prime ministers turned to Jane Austen for relief in troubled times. During the Second World War, while recovering from pneumonia, Sir Winston Churchill asked his daughter to read to him: "I had long ago read Jane Austen's *Sense and Sensibility*, and now I thought I would have *Pride and Prejudice*. Sarah read it to me beautifully from the foot of the bed. What calm lives they had, those people! No worries about the French Revolution, or the crashing struggle of the Napoleonic wars. Only manners

Read again and for the third time at least Miss Austen's very finely written novel of *Pride and Prejudice*. That young lady had a talent for describing the involvement and feelings and characters of ordinary life which is to me the most wonderful I ever met with. The Big Bow-wow strain I can do myself like any now going, but the exquisite touch which renders ordinary commonplace things and characters interesting from the truth of the description and sentiment is denied me. What a pity such a gifted creature died so early!
Sir Walter Scott, novelist, journal entry, March 14, 1826

controlling natural passion as far as they could, together with cultural explanations of any mischances."[3] In 11 Downing Street, Harold Macmillan read to control his anxiety, as he waited to hear of his accession to the premiership in 1957: "I passed the morning in the downstairs sitting-room and I read *Pride and Prejudice* – very soothing."[4] In the 19th century the Prime Minister Benjamin Disraeli claimed that he had read *Pride and Prejudice* seventeen times. If he too read it for its calming influence, maybe it was because no one in his Cabinet had any compassion for his poor nerves.

Festive mood
Costumed parades are all part of the Jane Austen Festival in Bath.

Festive mood
Regency dancing at the Jane Austen Festival in Bath. Right, men in their uniforms join the women in their bonnets.

TOP OF THE POLLS

In 2003, when the BBC conducted the largest-ever poll to discover the UK's best-loved book, *Pride and Prejudice* came second after *Lord of the Rings*. Two other surveys in the same year put Fitzwilliam Darcy in the number one slot. The first featured a list of fictional characters with whom women would most like to go on a date, with Jane Austen's smouldering hero edging James Bond and Superman into second and third place. The second survey compiled a list, in preferential order, of ten celebrity guests at a dinner party. Ahead of the Orange Prize for Fiction, again in 2003, *Pride and Prejudice* was voted the top book written by a woman, by female readers aged over 40. Significantly, women under 40 chose Helen Fielding's *Bridget Jones's Diary*, itself a modern take on *Pride and Prejudice*. In 2004, Radio 4 Woman's Hour listeners hailed *Pride and Prejudice* as the text most influential in changing women's perception of themselves. "If ever women wished to identify with a character, it must be Lizzy," claimed Monica Ali, the novel's champion. "She's quick-witted, lively, self-assured and yet so infallibly human and she takes us on that most important journey – the path to self-knowledge."[5] Another poll in 2007 voted *Pride and Prejudice* "the book the nation can't do without" and the following year a survey of more than 15,000 Australian readers placed it first on the roll call of the 101 best books ever written. Proof indeed, if any were needed, of the enduring quality of Jane Austen's light, bright, sparkling storyline and her endearing habit of completely trusting in her readers' intelligence and percipience. Wherever we live in the world, she persuades us to believe ourselves superior to those "dull elves, who have not a great deal of ingenuity themselves" for whom she definitely did not write *Pride and Prejudice*.

A Novel for All Time

Comedy of manners
'You must allow
me to present this
young lady to you.'

As we celebrate the bicentenary of this most beloved of Jane Austen's novels, it is instructive to ponder the reasons for its universal and timeless appeal. The truth is that *Pride and Prejudice* has everything: a satisfying love story, a delightful heroine, an array of memorable characters, witty dialogue and a narrator in sparkling form. And then there is the visual and social world that *Pride and Prejudice* conjures up, a world of elegant fashions, charming houses, exquisite manners and an accepted moral code. This too is beguiling, despite – or perhaps, because – the externals of our lives are so very different today. The novel can be interpreted afresh by every generation, and to judge by its popularity in universities as well as among general readers all over the world, it has something to say to all ages and all cultures.

The pace never slackens. Characters come and go as the author interweaves the progress of Elizabeth's relationships with both Wickham and Darcy, the subplot of Jane Bennet's on-off romance with Mr Bingley, the comedy of the ridiculous Mr Collins's search for a wife and, later in the book, the drama of Lydia's elopement and Elizabeth's ding-dong battle of wits with the interfering Lady Catherine de Bourgh.

Most of the action is seen through the eyes of Elizabeth Bennet as she endeavours to evaluate the individuals who come into her life. *Pride and Prejudice* proceeds without so much as a moment of tedium or verbosity, a rare achievement among 19th-century novels. It springs as freshly off the page as if it had been written yesterday, yet the elegance, irony and precision of its language transport us to a different age. It is a comedy of manners offering unchanging truths about human relationships; a novel for all seasons, that soothes and stimulates, amuses and fascinates: whatever our mood or our level of interest, it never lets us down.

"You must allow me to present this young lady to you"
Chap. VI.

A LOVE STORY

An inspired creation
Jennifer Ehle played Elizabeth Bennet in the BBC's 1995 adaptation of *Pride and Prejudice*.

Boy meets girl; because of the untoward circumstances of this meeting, they conceive an immediate dislike of one another; so blinding is the effect of this antagonism that for a while they refuse to acknowledge a mutually powerful attraction; as one advances in forgiveness and understanding, the other recedes, forming a dance-like pattern of courtship. The denouement comes when the man performs a selfless service for the woman, proving his true worth.

Both learn lessons about themselves which make them better people for the future, a strong new couple to carry their values into the next generation. Each has their reward in the true and tender love of a perfect soulmate; but the woman is also rewarded, Cinderella-like, with riches, a magnificent home and a high position in society. The conquest of a proud man's heart provides an additional *frisson*.

It is the stuff of which a thousand romance novels are made, a wish-fulfilment story, a fantasy perhaps, elevated by the skill of the author into a work of high art, inexhaustible in its layers of meaning. Unlike lesser examples of the genre, *Pride and Prejudice* can be read innumerable times and always yields new insights and new delights.

THE HEROINE

Elizabeth Bennet is an inspired creation. Jane Austen herself could not help admitting that she found her "the most delightful creature ever to appear in print". Most male readers fall a little in love with her and most female readers identify with her. This is perhaps because she stands up for herself and adheres to her own sense of right and wrong, whatever the pressures of society around her. She has to fend off the snobbery of others – the Bingley sisters, Lady Catherine de Bourgh – and withstand conventional demands on how she should behave by most of the people around her, including Mr Collins and her own mother. Mr Darcy's insult, on their first meeting, must seem like just another attack on her sense of self-worth and she uses her usual defences to laugh it off and to despise the perpetrator.

Like most young women of the period, Elizabeth has little money of her own and hardly any independence of action. She has to deploy all the stratagems at her disposal to secure a good life for herself. In circumstances unthinkable to today's women, she can neither leave her family home nor earn her own living; and she has to wait for men to make all the moves, leaving her with only the power of response.

But though she has little enough room for manoeuvre, Elizabeth is gifted with charm, spirit, wit and the optimism of youth. She is also physically attractive, with a light figure and fine dark eyes which

Unlike Jane's marriage to Bingley, Elizabeth's relationship with Darcy resonates with a physical passion the milder couple lacks. The rapport between these two from start to finish is intimate, even racy … Their arguments about personal motives or family embarrassments leave them more and more exposed to each other, and as a result more and more implicated in each other's trust. The fact that Darcy and Elizabeth form and pursue most of their relationship in secret and alone not only electrifies this intimacy, but also pushes it to the verge of an impropriety unique in Austen's fiction.
Claudia L. Johnson, *Jane Austen: Women, Politics and the Novel*, 1988

sparkle with intelligence and fun. Outspoken, opinionated and even subversive, yet highly principled, she is aware of the danger of being cleverer than most of the people around her. "I hope I never ridicule what is wise and good," she tells Darcy early in their acquaintance. "Follies and nonsense, whims and inconsistencies *do* divert me, I own, and I laugh at them whenever I can." She adds, in her teasing manner: "But these, I suppose, are precisely what you are without."

One of Elizabeth's most attractive qualities is her good humour and disposition to be happy – to make the best of things that she cannot alter. This is shown when her uncle and aunt change the itinerary of their holiday – in which Elizabeth is to accompany them – so that they will miss seeing the English Lake District, on which she has set her heart. "Elizabeth was excessively disappointed," we read. "But it was her business to be satisfied – and certainly her temper to be happy, and all was soon right again." And when the little party sets off, "One enjoyment was certain – that of suitableness as companions; a suitableness which comprehended health and temper to bear inconveniences, cheerfulness to enhance every pleasure, and affection and intelligence." These are the qualities, so important in daily life, that Elizabeth will bring to her role as wife and mother.

Until she marries, Elizabeth's closest relationship is with her elder sister, Jane. Though they share the same moral values, the sisters are very different in temperament. Elizabeth is much more acute and critical, Jane sees the best in everybody – but without being stupid. It is a measure of Elizabeth's generosity of spirit that she admires Jane without reservation and cares about her wellbeing almost as much as her own. One of the most delightful passages in the book occurs when Jane is taken ill at Netherfield and Elizabeth hastens to visit her, "crossing field after field at a quick pace, jumping over stiles and puddles with impatient activity, and finding herself at last in view of the house, with weary ankles, dirty stockings, and a face glowing with the warmth of exercise". Elizabeth's vitality is an intrinsic part of her charm, for the reader as well as for Mr Darcy.

THE HERO

Opinions are mixed about Darcy. In film and TV adaptations he is shown as handsome, brooding, virile: viewers can see his sexual attractiveness to women, whether played by Colin Firth, Matthew MacFadyen or Laurence Olivier. Despite – or even because of – some initial aloofness, he is a desirable mate and viewers are never in doubt that he will turn out to be the hero. In the book, his desirability is less obvious. Jane Austen has a difficult feat to carry off. She has to make her hero ultimately worthy of her heroine; but to begin with he must be unpleasant enough to alienate Elizabeth, not only by his initial rejection of her as a dancing partner, but right up to his badly-expressed first proposal of marriage – for a good third of the book, in fact. We love Elizabeth, so we dislike Darcy for being hurtfully rude and we are rooting for her when she scorns his insulting offer.

Darcy then does a rare thing: he listens to his adversary (Elizabeth) and takes on board what she says to the extent of changing himself – not his inner nature, which beneath his proud manner is an honourable one, but the way he regards and treats other people.

Artist's impression
The artist David White
has created his own view
of Elizabeth Bennet and
Mr Darcy, based on the
actors in the 1995 BBC
adaptation.

Playing Mr Darcy
David Rintoul, Colin Firth and Matthew Macfadyen are among the actors who have starred on screen as Jane Austen's hero.

He does this not knowing whether he will have a chance to woo Elizabeth again, but because he is convinced by her arguments and because he wants to be a better person. How many people would be capable of transforming themselves like this, rather than taking the simpler course of retreating into self-justification and defensiveness? It is most impressive, and endearing; but not everybody has found it plausible. Jane Austen knows that she must produce further evidence of Darcy's goodness – and she does.

First, there is the testimony of his housekeeper, who knows how humanely he runs his estate. Then, he puts himself to the trouble and expense of seeking out Wickham and bribing him to make an honest woman of Lydia Bennet, who has brought disgrace to the family. He does this in secret, without seeking any thanks, for love of Elizabeth, whose distress at Lydia's behaviour he has witnessed. While still ignorant of this unselfish act, and wrongly believing that Darcy will never ally himself now with anyone connected with Wickham, Elizabeth acknowledges to herself that Darcy "was exactly the man, who, in disposition and talents, would most suit her. His understanding and temper, though unlike her own, would have answered all her wishes. It was an union that must have been to the advantage of both; by her ease and liveliness, his mind might have been softened, his manners improved, and from his judgment, information and knowledge of the world, she must have received benefit of greater importance."

It is a rational, rather than a romantic, basis for marriage. Some readers have failed to be convinced that Elizabeth really is in love with Mr Darcy, and some have been inclined to take her at her word when she tells Jane that she began to fall in love with him on first seeing his magnificent grounds at Pemberley. In the book (as opposed to film and television) we may not quite warm to Darcy, or delight in his company, as we do with some other heroes of Jane Austen. He remains somewhat austere (but no less thrilling for that). We are satisfied that Elizabeth has found someone who will never bore her, and that though differing so much in demeanour, the couple are well-matched in intellect.

Nor need we fear that, in becoming his wife, Elizabeth's spirits – the happy, playful spirits that have made him fall in love with her – will be repressed. Her "lively, sportive manner" of talking to her husband causes young Georgiana Darcy some alarm until "she began to comprehend that a woman may take liberties with her husband, which a brother will not always allow in a sister more than ten years younger than himself".

20

A DYSFUNCTIONAL FAMILY

It was the stock in trade of novelists before Jane Austen to depict heroines who were orphans or separated by distance from their parents, obliged to make their way alone in a dangerous world. In *Pride and Prejudice* Jane Austen does something daringly new. She creates a credible, normal but dysfunctional family of two parents and their children, living an outwardly everyday existence, yet involving its own kind of problems for the heroine. It is one of the strokes of genius that set this novel above its predecessors in both realism and entertainment value.

Mr and Mrs Bennet are among the finest comic creations of English literature. The marriage of two such ill-assorted people is accounted for very plausibly. Twenty-three years ago the young Mr Bennet was taken in by Miss Gardiner's "youth and beauty, and that appearance of good humour, which youth and beauty generally

Comic creations
Mr and Mrs Bennet, as depicted by the artist Hugh Thomson.

"And this offer of marriage you have refused?"
Chap. XX

give". Soon finding himself saddled with a foolish, narrow-minded, self-pitying woman, from whom there is no escape, Mr Bennet looks to books and country pursuits (that is, the male-only pastime of shooting birds) for his solitary daily pleasures. His library is his private domain, where he can shut himself away from family hubbub. But in doing so he abdicates his responsibilities as a father, content merely to ridicule his children just as he ridicules his wife. Nor is his humour towards them indulgent, it is really quite cruel, though his repartee is couched in terms of mock-courtesy, which prevent his wife understanding him fully.

We cannot help liking him, however, for the clear sight and dry wit that only Elizabeth inherits. Mr Bennet has some of the funniest lines in the book. To put an end to the dreary piano-playing of his middle daughter, Mary, he tells her, "That will do, child. You have delighted us long enough." When Elizabeth steadfastly refuses Mr Collins's offer of marriage, and Mrs Bennet calls on her husband to "make Lizzy marry Mr Collins", Elizabeth is summoned to the library to hear what her father has to say on the subject – which is: "An unhappy alternative is before you, Elizabeth. From this day you must be a stranger to one of your parents. Your mother will never see you again if you do *not* marry Mr Collins, and I will never see you again if you *do*." Elizabeth can hardly help smiling, though the subject is a serious one for her. Towards the end of the book, when Darcy has asked for Elizabeth's hand only days after the engagement of Jane and Bingley, Mr Bennet concludes discussion of the subject with the remark: "If any young men come for Mary or Kitty, send them in, for I am quite at leisure."

In her witless replies to her husband, Mrs Bennet always comes off worse. Their exchanges have much of the highly polished artifice of stage dialogue. (The famous first chapter is composed almost entirely of dialogue, making it highly dramatic – as are many other scenes, which is why the novel translates so well to the screen.) Although we are meant to laugh at her, Mrs Bennet is almost too unpleasant to be comic. Her pressure on Elizabeth to marry the odious Mr Collins is one of her worse crimes, and her self-absorption under the shock of Lydia's elopement reduces still further any sympathy we may have felt towards her as the butt of her husband's jokes. She proves that she does not care who in the household suffers, as long as her own suffering is paramount. And then, when Wickham is bribed to marry Lydia, Mrs Bennet's joy is as unbounded as her recent bewailing. In all her emotions she has no sense of moderation or seemliness.

Some readers have objected to the great disparity in the characters

A father's words
'And this offer of marriage you have refused?'

Ah madam, what a relief it is to come back to your witty volumes, and forget the follies of today in those of Mr Collins and Mrs Bennet! How fine, nay how noble is your art in its delicate reserve, never insisting, never forcing the note, never pushing the sketch into the caricature!
Andrew Lang, *Letters to Dead Authors*, 1886

"In earnest contemplation"

Chap. XLIII

of the five sisters. Could they really belong to one family? Jane and Elizabeth are intelligent and well-judging; Lydia is a younger version of her mother, thoughtless and pleasure-seeking, with insipid Kitty trailing in her wake; while Mary, the plainest of them all, embarrasses them by her habit of showing off and spouting platitudes. Mary is nobody's favourite, excluded by the pairs of sisters above and below her in age. Is Elizabeth a tad unkind to Mary, making no attempt to be sisterly or to encourage her to better things? Some people have felt that Mrs Bennet should be Mr Bennet's *second* wife, so that Jane and Elizabeth are her stepdaughters. But not only is she inordinately proud of Jane's beauty, which she attributes to her own genes, but it is much more distressing for Elizabeth to feel ashamed of her *own* mother than of a conventional 'wicked stepmother'. Jane Austen chooses to make Elizabeth's tribulations belong to real life, rather than to literary convention.

MONEY AND MATRIMONY

Recent commentators have pointed out that Mrs Bennet is being a more responsible parent than Mr Bennet in seeking husbands for their daughters, since after his death they will be left without means of support. This is true; and perhaps, as a very youthful author when she created *Pride and Prejudice*, Jane Austen did not give due weight to the difficulties facing unmarried women in middle-age. Elizabeth seems not to entertain a moment's unease about her future, turning down not only Mr Collins's offer but Mr Darcy's first proposal, because it is worded in a manner that does not please her.

Her friend Charlotte Lucas is less idealistic, or perhaps less principled; certainly more pragmatic. She not only agrees to marry the pompous and servile clergyman Mr Collins, she actually encourages him to make her the offer. He comes to Longbourn to seek a wife among the five Bennet daughters, in obedience to the dictates of his patron, Lady Catherine de Bourgh, who has instructed him to "choose a gentlewoman for *my* sake, and for your *own*, let her be an active, useful sort of person, not brought up high, but able to make a small income go a good way". Mr Collins's eye alights naturally on the eldest daughter, Jane, but when Mrs Bennet drops a hint that Jane is on the verge of becoming engaged, "Mr Collins had only to change from Jane to Elizabeth – and it was soon done – done while Mrs Bennet was stirring the fire. Elizabeth, equally next to Jane in birth and beauty, succeeded her of course." And so Elizabeth is the lucky recipient of his clumsy, self-satisfied proposal of marriage. Fortunately she has the temerity to hold out against him, despite the

Elizabeth's tribulations
'In earnest contemplation.'

25

pressures put on her by her mother, and his own reluctance to take no for an answer.

Three days later Mr Collins finds a more willing recipient for his "love and eloquence" in Elizabeth's unromantic friend Charlotte Lucas who, at the age of 27 and without ever having been handsome, seizes her last chance to obtain a home and a husband of her own. Her reflections on her prospects provide a key passage in the book. "Mr Collins to be sure was neither sensible nor agreeable; his society was irksome, and his attachment must be imaginary. But still he would be her husband. Without thinking highly of either men or of matrimony, marriage had always been her object; it was the only honourable provision for well-educated young women of small fortune, and

Table of inspiration
Jane Austen's writing desk is on display at Jane Austen's House Museum.

however uncertain of giving happiness, must be their pleasantest preservative from want."

The other love interest in Elizabeth's life is George Wickham. He is so graceful, handsome and charming! With such open, friendly manners! So unlike Mr Darcy, with whom Elizabeth constantly compares him. Like half the female population of Meryton, Elizabeth is ready to fall in love with Wickham and, in believing the tales he tells her about the Darcy family, her prejudice against Mr Darcy is reinforced. When her aunt, Mrs Gardiner, warns her not to think of marriage to Wickham, as neither of them has enough money to live on, Elizabeth concedes the point. She is sensible enough to admit that money is a prerequisite to marriage, and robust enough not to suffer from a broken heart. Wickham next pursues a Miss King, who has just come into a fortune, which makes Mrs Gardiner fear he is mercenary. "Pray, my dear aunt," says Elizabeth, "what is the difference in matrimonial affairs, between the mercenary and the prudent motive? Where does discretion end, and avarice begin? Last Christmas you were afraid of his marrying me, because it would be imprudent; and now, because he is trying to get a girl with only ten thousand pounds, you want to find out that he is mercenary." It is a good question, and one with which *Pride and Prejudice* is much concerned.

For all his deceptively gentle ways, Wickham turns out to be a serial seducer of young ladies, a spendthrift, a gamester and a liar. His punishment in finding himself the husband of the frightful Lydia Bennet is poetic justice. There is perhaps a little of the story-book villain about Wickham, but without him Elizabeth's journey to self-knowledge would be less testing, less colourful and less convincing.

Darcy's her strongest and most charismatic character. For generations of middle-class English schoolgirls, he has been the great romantic hero. They have fantasies about sleeping with Heathcliff, but it is Darcy they want to marry. "A fine, tall person, handsome features, noble mien …" And all that money! It's like Mills and Boon translated into English. Max Davidson, *The Daily Telegraph*, September 22, 1995

Jane Austen's own darling child

Two remarkable facts about *Pride and Prejudice* are that it was turned down by the first publisher to whom it was offered; and that Jane Austen made less money from it than from any other book published during her lifetime. She began to write an early version of *Pride and Prejudice* in October 1796, shortly before her 21st birthday, finishing it in August 1797, aged 21½. It is an astonishing feat. At this stage, it may or may not have been a novel told in the form of letters, like the *Elinor and Marianne* (forerunner of *Sense and Sensibility*) that she had recently completed, and various fragments written in her teenage years including the audacious novella *Lady Susan*. In *Pride and Prejudice* as we know it, 44 letters are mentioned, quoted or given in full; Elizabeth would have had several useful correspondents in her sister Jane, her aunt Mrs Gardiner and her married friend Charlotte Collins, besides other characters who could plausibly carry on the story by writing to one another. But scholars are divided on this point, and we can never know now.

In whatever form it stood, it was a fully finished novel, good enough in her father's view to submit to a publisher. Three months after its completion, and after it had been much read and admired among the family, the Rev. George Austen wrote on his daughter's behalf to the publisher Cadell, inquiring whether they would like him to send for their perusal "a manuscript novel, comprising 3 vols., about the length of Miss Burney's *Evelina*". Whether Mr Austen chose to mention *Evelina* because it too is a novel told in letters, or because when published in 1778 it was a runaway best-seller, and he was hoping to encourage a favourable response by association, his ploy failed. Cadell wrote back by return declining to even to look at the manuscript. It must be the missed opportunity of all time.

Daughter and father
Jane Austen was depicted in a pencil and watercolour sketch by her sister Cassandra (c.1810). Below, the Rev. George Austen.

FIRST IMPRESSIONS

Austen's title at this time was *First Impressions*. It is an excellent title, well suited to the theme and plot of her book, since they spring from the first impressions that Elizabeth forms of both Fitzwilliam Darcy and George Wickham, leading her so spectacularly astray and requiring the whole story to correct. The phrase was in common usage at the time, appearing in works by two of Austen's favourite authors, Ann Radcliffe and Samuel Richardson, where it acts as a warning against falling in love at first sight. There is also the aspect of Elizabeth's 'first impressions' of picturesque landscape when she goes travelling up north, a burlesque on the 1790s vogue for travel writing that may have been curtailed in later revisions.

Walking dress
A fashionable outfit that might have made a good first impression.

Cadell's rejection put a stop to Jane Austen's hopes of publication for several years. As far as we know, no other publisher was approached by Mr Austen, who seems to have given up easily. However, we cannot be absolutely certain about this, as it is only by fluke that his letter, endorsed "declined by Return of Post" was found within the firm's archives seventy years later. (It is also just possible that Jane never knew of her father's approach, and that he had been hoping to give her a pleasurable surprise.)

While she got on with writing her next book (the novel that would be published after her death as *Northanger Abbey*) the story of Elizabeth and Darcy continued to entertain her family and friends. "I do not wonder at your wanting to read 'First Impressions' again, so seldom as you have gone through it, and that so long ago," Jane wrote to her sister Cassandra, who was then staying with their brother Edward in Kent, in January 1799. In June that year Jane was on holiday in Bath, while Cassandra remained at home and was visited by their friend Martha Lloyd. Martha had evidently requested to read the manuscript again, or perhaps had suggested it for reading aloud as their evening entertainment. But Jane must have taken the manuscript with her, or locked it away and taken the key. She responded jokingly to Cassandra: "I would not let Martha read 'First Impressions' again upon any account, and am very glad that I did not leave it in your power. She is very cunning, but I see through her design; she means to publish it from memory, and one more perusal must enable her to do it."

It was perhaps inevitable that somebody else would get in first with such a good title. In 1801 a novel called *First Impressions* by Margaret Holford appeared — sunk now, without trace. If she ever hoped to publish her own manuscript, Jane would have to seek an alternative title for her work.

In the same year as this setback the Austen family – parents, and two unmarried daughters – left their Hampshire rectory, where Jane had spent her first 25 years, and moved to Bath, renting a house in Sydney Place. The upheaval, the busy social life and lack of privacy of a town, the death of Mr Austen in 1805, and the subsequent removal from one set of lodgings to another, first in Bath and then in Southampton, all contributed to a long hiatus in Jane's writing career. It was not until 1809, when the sisters and their mother moved to Chawton Cottage, on the Hampshire estate of her wealthy brother Edward, that Jane felt settled enough to embark again on any sustained writing – and this time with a fresh determination to be published.

A CHANGE OF TITLE

The phrase PRIDE AND PREJUDICE, printed in capitals, occurs three times in a single paragraph at the end of *Cecilia* (1782), by one of Jane Austen's favourite writers, Fanny Burney. Jane must have known of it long before she chose the title *First Impressions*, but now turned to it as a pleasing alternative. It has the merits of being alliterative, and good shorthand for the faults that keep hero and heroine apart for the best part of three volumes. We who love the novel cannot think of it as anything else but *Pride and Prejudice*, but for Jane and her family the change must have taken some getting used to.

Brotherly affection
Henry Austen, a prosperous banker, helped to arrange the first publication of *Pride and Prejudice*.

The new title also chimes well with *Sense and Sensibility*, the first novel that Austen sent out into the world from Chawton Cottage, published late in 1811. With the help – certainly practical, and possibly financial – of her brother Henry, at that time a prosperous London banker and man of the world, she entered into an arrangement with the publisher Thomas Egerton to publish her first novel 'on commission'. This meant that she undertook to reimburse Egerton if the edition made a loss, but that conversely, any profit was hers to keep after costs of printing, advertising and a ten per cent commission were deducted. This was not quite vanity publishing, and was a perfectly respectable procedure adopted even by many well-known authors at the time. It carried a slight risk, but one which Henry presumably encouraged her to take, perhaps promising to help her out if necessary; Henry was a born optimist. Jane Austen's personal allowance was little more than £20 per year, but she had received a legacy of £50 in 1807, which she perhaps held in reserve. In the event, the first edition of

Sense and Sensibility sold out, making her a clear £140 – the first money that she had earned in her life. The double gratification of earning money and seeing her work in print, after all the years of frustration, must have been immense.

At the same time she was evidently busy revising *First Impressions* into the *Pride and Prejudice* that we know today. The extent of her revision is impossible to gauge, since no manuscript of either version remains. All we can be sure of, in Jane's own words, is that "I have lop't and crop't so successfully ... that I imagine it must be rather shorter than S.&S. altogether". (It is.) The tone of *Pride and Prejudice* is so youthful and joyous – notwithstanding a dash of cynicism and a fair dose of irony – that it seems to read very largely as the production of a 21-year-old author, albeit an extraordinarily gifted one, at once exuberant and highly controlled.

So perfect for its purpose is the text of *Pride and Prejudice* that we can only be thankful that the early manuscript *was* rejected by Cadell in 1797, giving the author the opportunity to apply whatever second thoughts her greater experience of life and literature suggested. *Pride and Prejudice* as we have it is a matchless blend of youthful fun and mature judgment.

PRAISE AND PEWTER

Jane Austen sent *Pride and Prejudice* to Egerton before the full success of her first novel was known. She was keen that, rather than publish on commission again, he should buy the copyright. Now dealing with a proven author he offered £110; she accepted, though she had estimated its value at £150. "Its being sold will I hope be a great saving of Trouble to Henry, & therefore must be welcome to me," she wrote to Martha Lloyd in November 1812. "The Money is to be paid at the end of the twelvemonth." She does not sound very triumphant. By selling the copyright, she knew that she would make no further profit from this, the novel which, if her own family and friends were anything to go by, she had every reason to suppose would prove more popular than her first. Made for the most unselfish of reasons, it was a sad decision, which came to seem even more regrettable when *Sense and Sensibility* went into a second edition, bringing further profit over the next few years. It has been calculated that had she proceeded on the same basis as before, *Pride and Prejudice* would have brought her about £475 in her lifetime, after costs.

Money was very important to Jane Austen – because she had so little of her own, and therefore so little independence of action or security for the future. She deplored being dependent on the

> But now comes the greatest miracle of English Literature. Straight on the heels of *Lady Susan* and *Sense and Sensibility* this country parson's daughter of barely twenty-one breaks cover with a book of such effortless mastery, such easy and sustained brilliance, as would seem beyond the reach of any but the most mature genius. *Pride and Prejudice* has probably given more perfect pleasure than any other novel.
> Reginald Farrer, *Quarterly Review*, July 1917

Chawton Cottage
The house where Jane Austen revised the text of her 'darling child'.

generosity of her brothers who, though kind, had families and money worries of their own. "I have now written myself into £250, which only makes me long for more," she wrote to her brother Francis, a British naval officer, when the first edition of *Sense and Sensibility* sold out; and on another occasion, lamenting the tendency of people to borrow rather than buy, "I like praise as much as anybody, but I like what Edward calls Pewter too".

Even so, money was not the only, or the chief, consideration in publishing. In January 1813 Cassandra was visiting their brother James in Steventon when Jane wrote excitedly: "I want to tell you that I have got my own darling Child from London." More than fifteen years after it was first offered to a publisher, she proudly held in her hands the three volumes of *Pride and Prejudice* in print.

She also had the pleasure of seeing her work advertised in *The London Morning Chronicle*, at a cost of 18 shillings (90p). But her name did not appear anywhere. At the turn of the 19th century it was the convention to publish fiction anonymously, certainly when it was by a woman, but sometimes even by men. The title page of *Pride and Prejudice* said "By the author of Sense and Sensibility", which itself had been published simply as "By a Lady".

A Chawton neighbour, Miss Benn, happened to dine with her mother and herself on the very day that the precious volumes arrived. "In the evening we set fairly at it, and read half the first vol. to her," Jane told Cassandra. Oh lucky Miss Benn – impoverished spinster though she was, with a rather miserable existence, on this occasion who would not envy her? The two Austen women concealed the secret of Jane's authorship. "I believe it passed with her unsuspected. She was amused, poor soul! *That* she could not help, you know, with two such people to lead the way, but she really does seem to admire Elizabeth. I must confess that I think her as delightful a creature as ever appeared in print, and how I shall be able to tolerate those who do not like *her* at least I do not know."

In her next letter to Cassandra, however, Jane confessed to having had "some fits of disgust" at her own work – a common reaction in writers. "Our 2nd evening's reading to Miss Benn had not pleased me so well, but I believe something must be attributed to my Mother's too rapid way of getting on – & tho' she perfectly understands the Characters herself, she cannot speak as they ought," Jane wrote wryly. But she added, "Upon the whole however I am quite vain enough & well satisfied enough."

OPINIONS

Reactions from friends and family began to flow in. "Fanny's praise is very gratifying," Jane told Cassandra of a niece. "Her liking Darcy & Elizth is enough. She might hate all the others, if she would." "Lady Robert is delighted with P&P – and really was so as I understand before she knew who wrote it – for of course, she knows now." Henry, in his brotherly pride, had been giving the game away, especially to his well-connected friends. "I long to have you hear Mr H's opinion of P&P. His admiring my Elizabeth so much is particularly welcome to me." Mr H was Warren Hastings, the retired Governor-General of Bengal and a friend of the Austen family. "I am quite delighted with what such a man writes about it."

She would certainly have been delighted had she known that another eminent man, the playwright Richard Brinsley Sheridan, was urging his dinner companions to buy *Pride and Prejudice* immediately, "for it was one of the cleverest things he had ever read".[6] The young lady who recorded this, a Miss Shirreff, took his advice and became an equally avid admirer. Appreciation of Elizabeth Bennet as a character new to fiction was widespread; a large element of the readers' delight focused on her, just as Jane Austen had wished. Among reviews that appeared at the time of publication, *The Critical Review* felt that

Superficially, in *Pride and Prejudice*, Jane Austen is describing a world that has vanished. Go below the surface, however, and she is coming close to people, with their absurd hopes and fears, their little meannesses and acts of generosity, as they still are today... Real women are much better, altogether more satisfying, than dream figures; and Elizabeth Bennet is one of the first and best of them in fiction, not only in English but all fiction.
J. B. Priestley, *Literature and Western Man*, 1960

"Elizabeth's sense and conduct are of a superior order to those of the common heroines of novels", and *The British Critic* found her character to be "supported with great spirit and consistency throughout; there seems no defect in the portrait". These reviewers were male; the female population were just as likely to be thrilled by Darcy. Annabella Milbanke, a fashionable young lady, wrote to her mother that the novel was "a very superior work", and that "the interest is very strong, especially for Mr Darcy".[7] She would soon have her own dashing hero in her life (much good it did her) in the shape of Lord Byron, whose wife she became.

Even the Prince Regent bought a set of the three volumes for each of his residences. It is hard to think of the roistering Prince doing anything as quiet as reading a novel, let alone sympathising with characters belonging to the minor country gentry; but he professed himself a devotee of all Jane Austen's works. (She did not return the compliment, deploring the Prince's lifestyle.)

With the help of favourable reviews and word of mouth among the great and the good, the first edition of *Pride and Prejudice* (probably 1,000 copies) sold out in nine months. Egerton brought out a second edition in October 1813. Though the author received no financial benefit from this, she must have been delighted that her darling child was proving so popular as to require a reprint within the same year.

As her later novels became published, Jane Austen began to keep a written record of what her friends and family said about them, under the title 'Opinions'. She had kept no such record of the reception of *Pride and Prejudice*, but the title cropped up many times in people's responses to her later work, which Jane extracted both from letters and from direct and reported conversation. For example, of *Mansfield*

"So much love and eloquence"

Park, "We certainly do not think it as a whole, equal to P&P – but it has many great beauties," wrote her brother Francis. "Not so clever as P&P," opined her brother Edward, while his two eldest sons had "Not liked it near so well as P&P". Jane's mother also "Not liked it so well as P&P", while Cassandra "thought it quite as clever, tho' not so brilliant, as P&P". Jane's friend Anne Sharp, who had once been governess to Edward's daughters, had praise for *Mansfield Park*, "but as you beg me to be perfectly honest, I must confess I prefer P&P". Jane's niece Anna was one of the few who "liked it better than P&P". The most amusing response was that of a neighbour Mrs Augusta Bramston, who "owned that she thought S&S and P&P downright nonsense, but expected to like MP better, & having finished the 1st vol. flattered herself she had got through the worst". Jane must have laughed as she committed that to paper.

Well received
Mr Collins proposes to Charlotte Lucas. Above, the first edition of *Pride and Prejudice* was published in three volumes.

When *Emma* came out in 1816, people were still finding *Pride and Prejudice* hard to beat: "My mother thought it more entertaining than MP but not so interesting as P&P. No characters in it equal to Lady Catherine and Mr Collins." Mrs Austen evidently had a taste for high comedy. Jane's uncle, James Leigh Perrot, and his wife "saw many beauties in it [*Emma*] but could not think it equal to P&P. Darcy & Elizth had spoilt them for anything else". A Mrs Dickson "did not much like it – thought it very inferior to P&P". Jane Austen was all too aware of the dangers of raising expectations in her readers that might not be fulfilled. When people have enjoyed a novel they usually want more of the same, and are indignant or disappointed when the author attempts something new. To her brother Frank she had written of having a new work on hand – *Mansfield Park* – "which I hope on the credit of P&P will sell well, tho' not half so entertaining". When *Emma* appeared, Austen confessed "I am very strongly haunted with the idea that to those readers who have preferred *Pride and Prejudice* it will appear inferior in wit, and to those who have preferred *Mansfield Park* very inferior in good sense".

At the time of publication, as we have seen, referring to her heroine she had said darkly: "How I shall be able to tolerate those who do not like *her* at least I do not know." There was one such person, but fortunately Jane did not know that Mary Russell Mitford, twelve years younger and herself an author, wrote in 1814 a letter to a friend deploring "the entire want of taste which could produce so pert, so worldly a heroine as the beloved of such a man as Darcy".[8] Miss Mitford, like Jane Austen the daughter of a Hampshire clergyman, was out of step with everybody else.

The Afterlife of a Masterpiece

N ine years after the railway cut through Jane Austen's part of Hampshire in 1840, *Pride and Prejudice* was listed as No.10 in The Railway Library series, published by George Routledge and Co., Soho Square. No copies exist today, so presumably they were flimsy in construction, although it's somehow satisfying to imagine them falling to pieces in the hands of early Austen addicts, perhaps travelling on the trains between London and Alton. In the mid-1880s Routledge produced another two cheap editions; one carried an illustration of Mr Collins's proposal and advertisements for patent medicines, the other was a Routledge's *Sixpeny Novel*. Times were changing out of all recognition, but Jane Austen's "darling child" was gathering speed too and would not be left behind in the past.

Charlotte Brontë probably hoped that it would be flattened on the rails. In the 1840s the critic G. H. Lewes had recommended that she read the novel, which she duly did, afterwards writing with asperity: "… I got the book. And what did I find? An accurate daguerrotyped portrait of a commonplace face; a carefully-fenced, highly-cultivated garden, with neat borders and delicate flowers … I should hardly like to live with her ladies and gentlemen, in their elegant but confined houses."[9] She later asserted that "the passions were perfectly unknown" to Jane Austen, a claim we find odd today, given our modern interpretation of the palpable attraction between Darcy and Elizabeth. "It's clear that Darcy very early on has the hots for Elizabeth Bennet … there she is, running about everywhere. It's quite obvious she would be wonderful in bed," is the opinion of the screenwriter Andrew Davies. D. H. Lawrence, who grumbled into his beard that Jane Austen was "a narrow gutted spinster", would have been "all astonishment".

Modern interpretation
The screenwriter Andrew Davies, below at a Jane Austen convention, is responsible for putting Mr Darcy (Colin Firth) in the famous wet shirt.

The first publication to exploit Jane Austen's potential as a high-earning author, rather than a sixpenny throwaway, was George Allen's 1894 edition of *Pride and Prejudice*. This was a consciously plush production, in blue-green cloth, with a gilt peacock design on the front board and spine. What made it even more special were the 160 line drawings for which the illustrator, Hugh Thomson, was paid £500, plus a royalty payment of sevenpence for every copy sold over 1,000. He earned more money from this edition than the author or any of her family ever had. In just one year 11,605 copies had been sold, plus another 3,500 that were sent to America. By 1907 that number had reached 25,000. George Saintsbury, the revered academic and critic who wrote the preface, revealed endearingly that he had fallen hopelessly in love with Elizabeth Bennet. Thomson's drawings achieved iconic status, so much so that they are still instantly recognisable today. Many visitors to Jane Austen's House Museum in Chawton will have seen the first set of printers' proofs for *Pride and Prejudice* displayed on the first floor landing. Jane Austen's second novel had acquired the distinction of collector's item.

Encouraged by the phenomenal popularity of Hugh Thomson's illustrations, the artist Charles E. Brock wrote a letter to Macmillan and Co promising to deliver drawings for yet another illustrated version of *Pride and Prejudice*. This lavish edition came out in 1895, printed on the best quality gilt-edged paper and featuring a frontispiece and 39 plates printed alongside the text, all but one full-page. *Pride and Prejudice* was not only thought worthy of superior paper; eminent critics began to value it too. W. D. Howells, the American novelist and critic, claimed that the novel had created an Austen cult and turned its author into "a passion and a creed, if not quite a religion".[10] For his friend and fellow novelist Mark Twain, however, the idea of a divine Jane Austen turned him into an iconoclast: "Every time I read *Pride and Prejudice* I want to dig her up and hit her over the skull with her own shin-bone."[11] Yet it is worth noting that this particular novel held a horrid fascination for him, because he implies that he could not resist reading and re-reading it.

In the 20th century publication continued apace. As a result of serious critical attention the novel began to appear on the school curriculum and a number of abridged versions were produced for use in the classroom, some quite severely reduced: the 1910 Cambridge University Press version was half the novel's original length, that produced by Macmillan & Co in 1917 retained only 26 of 61 chapters. One abridged edition in 1942 sacrilegiously omitted the first sentence. Most included mind-numbing exercises at the back:

Plush production
Hugh Thomson's line drawings for *Pride and Prejudice* were first seen in George Allen's edition with its gilt peacock design. Examples can be seen on pages 21 and 40.

"Discuss in no more than 500 words why Elizabeth is prejudiced and Darcy proud …" Some publishers lumped *Pride and Prejudice* in with other, often incongruous, texts – *Jane Eyre*, *Cranford*, *Silas Marner*, *A Sentimental Journey*, *Wuthering Heights*, for example.

The 1923 Oxford Clarendon Press edition of *Pride and Prejudice*, edited by the eminent Austen scholar R. W. Chapman and reprinted throughout the century, is still referenced in many studies today. One thousand sets of all of the novels were printed initially, each one including illustrations from contemporary sources rather than imaginary representations of the characters. This was the first scholarly edition of any English novelist and Chapman's meticulous research led to Jane Austen's acceptance into the hallowed realm of academe. In actual fact, it was Chapman's wife, Katharine Metcalfe, who had first taken a serious critical interest in *Pride and Prejudice*. Her edition of the novel, with quotes from past critics and notes detailing Austen's life and times, came out in 1912, the year that she met her future husband. It seems somehow fitting that they fell in love over *Pride and Prejudice*, less fitting that Chapman omitted to acknowledge in print his wife's contribution to the 1923 edition. A scholarly approach to *Pride and Prejudice* has been further developed by Cambridge University Press, which published a fully annotated edition of the novel in 2006. This definitive study covers context and publication history and includes a chronology of Jane Austen's life, authoritative textual commentaries and explanatory notes.

Editions and sequels
Stolz und Vorurteil is the German title of *Pride and Prejudice*. Right, from the top, Ava Farmer (also known as Sandy Lerner), Carrie Bebris and P. D. James have all written follow-ups to the book.

American editions of the novel became more prevalent from the 1930s onwards. The 1940 Hollywood film promoted a "special film edition", featuring stills inside and on the dustwrapper. In 1961, the year that Yuri Gagarin became the first man in space, *Pride and Prejudice* was first published in Moscow. The novel's translation from English into Russian followed six years later. Throughout the 20th century foreign translations of the novel increased, especially after the Second World War. An early German translation, *Stolz und Vorurteil*, came out in 1830, followed by a second in 1939. A pre-war French edition re-named the novel *Les cinq filles de Mrs Bennet*, but then reverted to the more usual *Orgueil et préjugés*. Now, *Pride and Prejudice* can be read and enjoyed in languages as diverse as Chinese and Telegu, Sinhalese and Swedish.

SEQUELS AND SPIN-OFFS

Sequels, prequels and variations are 'translations' of a different order. "Give a loose to your fancy, indulge your imagination in every possible flight which the subject will afford," writes Elizabeth Bennet to her Aunt Gardiner. Her invitation could, with as much relevance, be applied to modern creators of fictions inspired by *Pride and Prejudice*. The proliferation of such works since 1995 has been phenomenal; more than 300 titles appear on internet lists, a handful up to this date, hundreds after. Some authors go in for a scatter effect, drawing on characters from all of the novels to populate their fictions, as Sybil G. Brinton did in 1913, in the earliest sequel, *Old Friends and New Fancies*, where romantic alliances are made between, for example, Mary Crawford and Colonel Fitzwilliam, Georgiana Darcy and William Price. Ava Farmer's *Second Impressions* (2012) uses the same technique. Lily Adams Beck's *The Darcys of Rosings* (1922) adopted a more conservative approach, taking only the characters and locations from *Pride and Prejudice* and other authors followed her lead.

Now, writers of all kinds turn their minds to a myriad of possible, not always plausible, scenarios – *Pride and Prejudice on Mars* and *Fitzwilliam Darcy: Rock Star* have to be the most improbable on the list. Jane Austen's characters venture into the realm of the undead, with Mr Darcy more often than not leading the way, in fantasies such as *Vampire Darcy's Desire* and *Mr Darcy's Bite*. Soft porn is also on the agenda; titles such as *Pride and Prejudice: Hidden Lusts*, *Pride and Prejudice: The Wild and Wanton Edition* and *Darcy and Elizabeth: Nights and Days at Pemberley*, explore the main characters' basic and not-so-basic sexual urges. Some authors focus on the theme of oppositional duality: *Drive and Determination*, *Duty and Desire*, *Virtue and Vanity*; while others expand the histories of minor characters: *Lydia Bennet's Story*, *There's Something About Mary Bennet* and *Deborah*, the persona Anne De Bourgh assumes after she has run away from Rosings.

A number of writers choose to give an insight into Darcy's – and it is invariably Darcy's – mindset, from his first appearance at Meryton, sometimes farther back in time, to his marriage. This is achieved by way of diaries, confessions or memoirs. Many concentrate on the married life of the Darcys, imagining the "connubial felicity" that Lizzy predicted for herself and her husband, or describing marital infidelities and recriminations; some create a Pemberley filled with children, others make the Darcys infertile. The American writer Carrie Bebris constructs an entirely different kind of life for Elizabeth and Darcy. She turns them into "reluctant sleuths" and sends them off to Northamptonshire to solve *The Matters at Mansfield*, or to Surrey to

uncover *The Intrigue at Highbury*. "Mr Darcy as a detective makes him pretty much the perfect hero," states the author, and P. D. James, the doyenne of detective fiction, must have felt the same when she decided to write *Death Comes to Pemberley*. Love them or hate them, for huge numbers of readers and writers the prequels, sequels and variations on the original fulfil a craving to squeeze as much pleasure as possible out of *Pride and Prejudice*.

TV AND FILM

In May 1938, when the transmitter at Alexandra Palace in London had a guaranteed range of only 25 miles and few people had access to television, the BBC aired a 55-minute *Pride and Prejudice*. Seven actors and seven actresses managed to fill all the parts. According to *The Times* newspaper, this "charming" production was broadcast twice, which meant two live performances because pre-recording at this time was not technologically possible.

The first professional film adaptation of the novel, directed by Robert Z. Leonard was released by MGM in 1940. It starred Laurence Olivier and Greer Garson, at 35 probably the oldest actress to play Elizabeth. "It happened in OLD ENGLAND" were the opening words flashed on to the big screen, evoking a time of moral and traditional certainties, untroubled by the threat of bombs and the death of thousands at home and abroad. For a wartime audience

First adaptations
Greer Garson and Laurence Olivier starred in the 1940 MGM version. Right, Jane Austen's letter to Cassandra in which she refers to her 'darling child'.

..., poor soul. That she is not deep you know, which is not
to lead the way; but she really does seem to admire
not confess that I think her as delightful a creature as e
...ed in print, & how I shall be able to tolerate those who
her at least, I do not know. — There are a few Typical
said he" or a "said she" would sometimes make the Dial
...ediately clear — but I do not write for such dull Elves
"As have not a great deal of Ingenuity themselves." —
...ster than I do wish — but the difference is not so much
look., there is very ... a proportion of Narrative in the
...e lost & c ... that I imagine

2
Chawton, Friday

I hope you received my little parcel
...day even, my dear Cassandra, & that you w...
me again on Sunday, for I feel that I must
Your parcel is safely arrived & everything sha
Thank you for your note. As you had not t...
...time it was very good in you to write, but
your debtor soon. — I want to tell you that
darling child from London; on Wednesday I
down by Falknor, with three lines from Henr...
given another to Charles & sent a 3d by the
first the two Sets which I was least eager fo...
I wrote to him immediately to beg for my l...
he would take the trouble of forwarding the
...enton & Portsmouth — not having an idea o...
before to day; by your account however he wa...
Letter was written. The only evil is the dela...
can be done till his return. Till James is r...
Love. — For your sake I am as well pleased
...ght be unpleasant to you to be in the...
...e do at the first burst of the business.

desperately in need of a happy, uncomplicated ending, whole swaths of the novel were either omitted or ruthlessly simplified. Jane Austen's Lady Catherine, candid to the point of rudeness and interfering beyond endurance, was transformed from control freak into concerned aunt, with the sole aim of testing Elizabeth's suitability as Darcy's wife: "She's right for you, Darcy. You were a spoiled child, but we don't want to go on spoiling you! What you need is a woman who will stand up to you. I think you've found her!"

Aldous Huxley, one of the scriptwriters, recognised that insistence on a purely comic approach, to the detriment of the ironic tone of the novel, was sure to result in "a major falsification of Miss Austen"[12] – a liberty that did not end with the indiscriminate alteration of character and plot. The huge success in 1939 of *Gone With the Wind* encouraged the director to set *Pride and Prejudice* in the 1840s, which allowed the costume designer to indulge herself with gigantic hats and voluminous crinolines. Through the dark years of fabric rationing, British women, reduced to short, straight skirts in unbecoming shades of brown, must have swooned over the iridescent oceans of silk and satin. Even in black and white the colours were almost tangible: "The shell-pink gauze muslin for Miss Jane, the blue for Miss Elizabeth." The set designer was less impressed. He had bought in, at huge expense, genuine Georgian tables and elegant chairs, only to see most of them swept aside and wrecked by an onslaught of uncontrollable frocks.

Three television series followed in the 1950s and 1960s, all six-parters, all predominantly theatrical in approach. In 1952 came the first of the BBC adaptations, paving the way for more productions over next four decades. Each one reflected the attitudes and fashions of the time. In the 1958 series Elizabeth Bennet was the cheeky, winsome girl-next-door; Darcy sported Olivier kiss-curls and disdainful upper lip. The 1967 Elizabeth was every inch a print-frocked Laura Ashley girl, complete with floppy Biba hat and false eyelashes; Darcy was given a collar-length footballer hairdo. Although none of these productions can compete with more recent screenings in terms of costume design, attention to period detail or naturalistic character portrayal, they were popular in their time and introduced *Pride and Prejudice* to a growing audience of BBC classic drama enthusiasts.

A decade empty of televised *Pride and Prejudice* followed; then, in 1980, came Fay Weldon's five-part BBC series, an episode shorter but almost an hour longer than previous adaptations. Still filmed largely in the studio under harsh lights and with fake gardens glimpsed through the windows, this version did, however, use period locations for

Making 'that' version
The directors of the BBC 1995 adaptation published a 'behind the scenes' book.

You fall in love with the characters instantly, and Jane Austen is such an amazing tease; she has a capacity to frustrate you in a very positive way. She'll place a series of possibilities in front of you and then divert you. Also, I hadn't realised how funny *Pride and Prejudice* is, how witty and light and how far from 'homework' it is to read.
Colin Firth, *The Making of Pride and Prejudice*, 1995

THE MAKING OF

PRIDE AND PREJUDICE

SUE BIRTWISTLE & SUSIE CONKLIN

external shots – Renishaw Hall in Derbyshire featured as Pemberley, Well Vale and Thorpe Tilney Hall in Lincolnshire were chosen for Netherfield and Longbourn. Elizabeth Garvie attracted much critical acclaim for her light, bright, sparkling Lizzy, and David Rintoul made a convincing Darcy, with his height and haughtiness. Lady Catherine exuded "dignified impertinence" from every pore, but her famous clash with Lizzy happened indoors, within the confines of the

Longbourn drawing room and lacked animation as a consequence. Mr Collins fulfilled Jane Austen's vision of a "tall, heavy-looking young man"; later adaptations have tended to favour shorter, slimmer actors. This version is often said to be preferred by Austen purists, in that Fay Weldon incorporates a sufficient amount of dialogue from the novel. Yet intrusive voice-overs and the embarrassing slapstick quality of added scenes, especially those featuring Mr Collins bumbling along with awkward gait to the strains of a bass clarinet, detract from those scenes that are more or less faithful to the text. In this light, omitting the movingly tender exchange between Elizabeth and her father after Darcy's second proposal is unforgivable. In any event, to a 1980s television audience this felt like the best screen production of *Pride and Prejudice* . . .

. . . And then, 15 years later, along came Andrew Davies and Sue Birtwistle to radically change the world's perception of *Pride and Prejudice* and to spark a revival of all things Austen. Unlike previous adaptations, the 1995 production was no low-budget offering. With £6 million in the moneybox, each of the six, hour-long episodes radiated period authenticity, no expense spared. Ten million UK viewers, more than the entire population of England and Wales when the novel was first published, became incurable addicts. Some 12,000 videos, released in the same week as the final episode, were sold in two hours; by the end of the following week 58,000 had been snapped up. Subsequent worldwide distribution resulted in the BBC netting an income well beyond the initial outlay. The decision was taken early on to make this adaptation on film, to create a more

Period authenticity
Left, Julia Sawalha as Lydia and Adrian Lukis as Wickham in the BBC's 1995 adaptation. Lyme Park, Cheshire, was Pemberley, the home of Darcy, in the same production.

fluid, less circumscribed stage-play effect than videotape. Period houses were carefully chosen to reflect the relative social positions of the characters, costumes and carriages selected to show their disposable incomes. The National Trust is still reaping the rewards of increased footfall in the properties featured, particularly Lyme Park (Pemberley) and Belton House (Rosings); the owners of Luckington Court (Longbourn) have benefited from a new roof.

Jane Austen, Andrew Davies claims, would recognise 80 per cent of the dialogue as her own – "We could just lift it out of the book." He realised that shorter adaptations had left out crucial scenes: "Her plot works just like a Swiss clock and doesn't have any flabby bits in it – everything counts".[13] This didn't prevent him from adding new scenes – Mr Collins encountering a scantily-clad Lydia on the stairs at Longbourn and most famously, or infamously, Mr Darcy diving into a pond and materialising unexpectedly in front of a transfixed Elizabeth. Davies justifies the wet-shirt scene persuasively: "In that brief moment, one is reminded that Darcy, for all his responsibilities as the owner of Pemberley, is actually a young man. And, by intercutting Elizabeth staring at his portrait with the flesh-and-blood Darcy the audience sees, one is able to point up the idea that there are many portraits of Darcy being formed in the story ..."[14]

Whatever Andrew Davies's reasoning, and despite – or most likely because of – accusations that he focused attention solely on the sexual charge between the hero and heroine, this production of *Pride and Prejudice* undoubtedly boosted sales of the novel. It generated an insatiable interest in the author's life and times too. The Jane Austen Centre in Bath opened its doors in 1999 to an influx of tourists, notably from the countries where the BBC series had been screened. Similarly, the cottage at Chawton, where Jane revised *Pride and Prejudice* for publication, enjoyed an exponential rise in its visitor numbers after 1995, from 30,000 to 56,000 a year. The elderly, the middle-aged, young adults, teenagers and those barely out of their cradles, all switched on to Jane Austen. A whole generation of children, now women in their twenties, watched the 1995 version repeatedly with their mothers and fell in love with the story and the characters. Here is one 12-year-old *Pride and Prejudice* fan describing her progression from TV adaptation to book: "I became hooked on Jane Austen when I saw the BBC's *Pride and Prejudice*, with Jennifer Ehle and Colin Firth. I fell in love with its witty lines, the romantic encounters and the absolutely beautiful costumes. I've now seen it six times and I've also read the book – I found the language quite hard at times but it is still one of the best novels I've read."[15]

Cashing in on Jane
Martin Salter is a familiar face in Bath, standing outside the Jane Austen Centre with 'Lizzy' to welcome visitors.

INTO THE 21ST CENTURY

How many new readers searched the pages in vain for an erotically damp Mr Darcy is unrecorded, but their disappointment need not be lasting. "Jump into the pond … You know you want to" is the advertising strap-line of P and P Tours, set up in 2007 on the strength of the 1995 series to cater for *Pride and Prejudice* location seekers from all over the world. Since the tours began, proposals of marriage have been made at "Hunsford Parsonage", Mr Beveridge's Maggot danced in the hall at "Longbourn" ("Only we can take you there …") and the banks of the celebrated pond thronged by virile young men, shirts on or off, ready to perform that iconic dive for the clicking cameras.

Jumping into the bottomless commercial pond created by the 1995 adaptation has become a regular occupation for novelists, film makers and sequel writers. Helen Fielding's *Bridget Jones's Diary*, published in 1996, filmed in 2001, covers the year of the Andrew Davies's production. At 8.55am, on Sunday, October 15, Bridget notes: "Just nipped out for fags prior to getting changed for BBC *Pride and Prejudice*. Hard to believe there are so many cars out on the roads. Shouldn't they be at home getting ready? Love the nation being so addicted. The basis of my own addiction, I know, is my simple human need for Darcy to get off with Elizabeth." Bridget is a thirtysomething singleton, experiencing an on-off relationship with the initially aloof, eminently eligible Mark Darcy (played by Colin Firth in the film) and a disastrous attraction to the manipulative rogue Daniel Cleaver. *Lost in Austen* (ITV, 2008) trades unashamedly and hilariously on the 1995 series. When Amanda Price, from modern-day Hammersmith, swaps places with Lizzy Bennet and finds herself in the time of Jane Austen's *Pride and Prejudice*, deconstructed mayhem follows. She tries to resist falling in love with Mr Darcy – "The whole world will hate me for it" – but fails dismally. When he reveals his love for her at Pemberley, Amanda pleads, "Will you do something for me?" Cut to the next scene, where a white-shirted Darcy rises from an ornamental lake. "I'm having a bit of a strange postmodern moment here," she admits.

Many questioned the sense of producing the most recent film of *Pride and Prejudice* (Universal Pictures / Working Title), starring Keira Knightley and Matthew Macfadyen. Ten years after the acclaimed televised production, a savagely "lop't & crop't" version was bound to disappoint and, at two hours in length, it captures only the basic outline of the plot and skimps on character development. Blink, and you miss Wickham altogether. On the plus side, the scenery is stunning and the musical score atmospheric. Jane Austen's dialogue

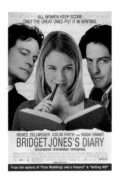

The commercial pond
Bridget Jones's Diary
covers the years
of Andrew Davies's
production of *Pride and Prejudice*. Right, even
Bollywood has joined in.

is apparent throughout, but blended with more modern expressions, delivered at a rapid pace and accompanied by manners more akin to the present age, with the acknowledged objective of attracting a different audience from that normally drawn to period movies. "The Politics of Dating" is the subject at the top of the Special Features list. The scene where Elizabeth tells her father of her love for Darcy is the most moving in the film; Elizabeth and Darcy together never come close to achieving the same level of emotional communication.

Locations leave a lot to be desired too. The choice of Chatsworth as Pemberley, leaving aside that Jane Austen makes reference to the Duke of Devonshire's extensive property on the Gardiners' tour itinerary, is completely misjudged, given Darcy's restrained, unostentatious taste. His income of £10,000, although a comfortable fortune, would also be insufficient to maintain such a large establishment. The Bennets' ramshackle farmhouse, complete with muddy yard and a pig in the hallway, creates a totally wrong impression of the family's social status. Perhaps that explains why this particular Elizabeth does not demand recognition as "a gentleman's daughter" when Lady Catherine descends on Longbourn, inexplicably in the middle of the night. Poor Darcy is unremittingly miserable from start to finish. The promise of conjugal felicity with Elizabeth doesn't appear to cheer him up one jot, even though she has walked across several misty fields in her nightdress to confess a change of heart. Mr Bingley's wayward hair threatens to sabotage

every scene in which it appears; his sister Caroline – there is no Mrs Hurst – is the only elegant female in the whole production. Kitty, Lydia and even Mrs Bennet herself invariably look dishevelled and not particularly fragrant – a strange state of affairs for a mother desperate to find husbands with money for all five daughters.

In 2004, Bollywood came up with its own tribute to *Pride and Prejudice*'s universal appeal. *Bride and Prejudice* gives Jane Austen's classic a modern twist in an Indian setting. The story follows the fortunes of the four daughters of the Bakshi family, who live in Amritsar. Lalita Bakshi is the heroine, Mr Darcy is the wealthy heir to an American hotel chain, and Wickham a student back-packer. Gurinder Chadha, the director, stresses her reliance on the novel: "Script editors told me to move away from the book, but I said no. I wanted to come back to the book at every turn."[16] She recognises the universal nature of Jane Austen's themes: "Our version may have different cultures and settings, but it's still about people marrying from different backgrounds ... It's very true to Jane Austen and the spirit of the book, and I think if she came down and went to see it in her local Odeon she would like it."

And we do wonder, don't we, how Jane Austen might react to the world's treatment of her "darling child". Would she still be capable of tracing its features despite extensive surgery? Could we ever hope to explain to her the fascination of a man in a wet shirt? Would she turn pale and faint on the nearest sofa if faced with *Pride and Prejudice and Zombies*, or laugh at the sheer light-hearted absurdity of it all? Given our love for her lightest, brightest, brilliantly sparkling jewel of a novel, she would surely forgive us our predilection for making of *Pride and Prejudice* whatever we will. Imitation, after all, is said to be the sincerest form of flattery.

The very first scene in the book, so gay, so funny, so famous, already indicates an emotional bleakness, in an undertone; for Mr Bennet is not bantering with his wife but privately laughing at her. Elizabeth and Darcy are never like this: there is a relationship, of a sort, between them from the start, even if it is a relationship of conflict ... One reason for [Darcy's] popularity is that he is the hero in whom sexual desire is most overt and overpowering. For what is he doing when he makes his first proposal to Elizabeth but telling her that he is so desperate to get her into bed that he will marry her even though it will be a degradation to him? The sexual charge is stronger in *Pride and Prejudice* than in any of the other novels, and that is a proper part of its character and appeal.
Richard Jenkyns,
A Fine Brush on Ivory,
2004

Postmodern moments
Elliot Cowan rises from
the lake in *Lost in Austen*.

Film and TV locations

Pemberley, home of Fitzwilliam Darcy
Lyme Park, Cheshire, 1995
Sudbury Hall, Derbyshire, 1995
Chatsworth House, Derbyshire, 2005

Longbourn, home of the Bennets
Luckington Court, Wiltshire, 1995
Groombridge Place, Kent, 2005

Rosings, home of Lady Catherine de Bourgh
Belton House, Lincolnshire, 1995
Burghley House, Lincolnshire, 2005
Stourhead, Wiltshire, 2005

Meryton, the Bennets' home town
Stamford, Lincolnshire, 2005
Lacock, Wiltshire, 1995

Netherfield Park, rented by Mr Bingley
Brocket Hall, Hertfordshire, 1995
Basildon Park, Berkshire, 2005
Edgecote Hall, Northamptonshire, 1995

Hunsford Parsonage, home of Mr Collins
Teigh, Rutland, 1995

Chatsworth House

Edgecote Hall

Luckington Court

Hunsford Parsonage

Lacock

Notes

Chapter One
1 *The Sunday Times*, October 17, 1999
2 *The Daily Telegraph*, March 27, 2011
3 Churchill, W. S., *The Second World War* (Cassell & Co, 1952)
4 Macmillan, H., *Riding the Storm* (Macmillan & Co, 1971)
5 BBC Online News December 8, 2004

Chapter Three
6 British Library MS 41253 f.17
7 Southam, B., *Critical Heritage* (1968) Vol. 1 p8
8 L'Estrange, A.G. (ed), *Life of Mary Russell Mitford* (1870) Vol. 1 p300

Chapter Four
9 Letter of January 12, 1848, to George Lewes
10 Southam, B., *Critical Heritage* (1968) Vol. 2 p227
11 Letter to Joseph Twichell, September 13, 1898
12 Letter to Eugene Saxton, 1939, in *Aldous Huxley* by Nicholas Murray
(Little, Brown, 2002)
13 Birtwistle, S., and Conklin, S., *The Making of Pride and Prejudice*
(BBC/Penguin, 1995)
14 ibid
15 *The Sunday Telegraph*, June 19, 2005
16 BBC Online News, October 4, 2004

Credits